750-799L

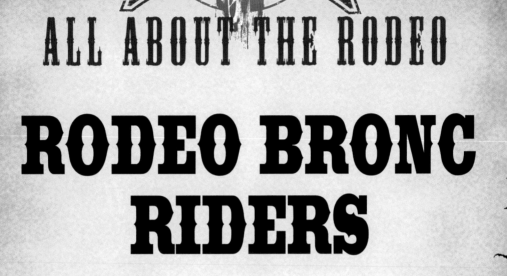

ALL ABOUT THE RODEO

RODEO BRONC RIDERS

Lynn Stone

Rourke
Publishing LLC
Vero Beach, Florida 32964

www.rourkepublishing.com

Photo credits:
Front cover © Eric Limon, back cover © Olivier Le Queinec, all other photos © Tony Bruguiere except page 8 © worldwide images, page 15 © Will Lowe, page 17 © Jim Parkin, page 23 © lightasafeather

Editor: Jeanne Sturm

Cover and page design by Nicola Stratford, Blue Door Publishing

Library of Congress Cataloging-in-Publication Data

Stone, Lynn M.
  Rodeo bronc riders / Lynn M. Stone.
     p. cm. -- (All about the rodeo)
  Includes index.
  ISBN 978-1-60472-388-5
  1. Bronc riding--Juvenile literature. 1. Title.
  GV1834.45.B75 S76 2009
  791.8/4 22
                            2008018791

Printed in the USA

CG/CG

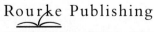

Rourke Publishing

www.rourkepublishing.com – rourke@rourkepublishing.com
Post Office Box 3328, Vero Beach, FL 32964

Table Of Contents

Rodeo Bronc Riders

So, you say you want your eggs scrambled? Try bronc riding. It's a rough and tumble ride that'll scramble anyone's breakfast.

Bronc riding is rodeo's classic sport, matching the strong will of a bucking horse, also known as a bronc, or **bronco**, against the equally strong will of a skilled rider. The bucking horse, of course, wants to throw the rider off. The rider is just as determined to finish the ride, which becomes official eight seconds after it begins, if the bronc rider can stay aboard that long. After eight seconds, there is still the matter of scrambling, or possibly being thrown, off the bronc's back. More often, a pickup man in the **arena** rides to the bronc and helps the rider to the ground.

Bareback bronc riders compete without saddles.

CHEYENNE FRONTIER DAYS
VOTED PRCA "LARGE OUTDO
RODEO OF THE YEAR"

Rodeo features two types of bronc riding, with saddles and without. Some competitors specialize in one kind or the other. Some compete in both forms.

Saddle bronc and bareback riding are generally men's events. They represent two of the three **roughstock**, or judged events, at major rodeos. The third is bull riding.

While his horse jumps for the sky, a tossed saddle bronc rider heads for the dirt.

Women find some competition in bronc riding events. The Women's Professional Rodeo Association (WPRA), for example, crowns a champion in bareback bronc riding but not in saddleback bronc.

Bronc riding is even more difficult than it sounds because of its style requirements. That is where the judging enters the equation, assuming a rider lasts for the official eight seconds in the first place.

Both horse and rider are judged on style.

Running the Events

The cowboy mounts the horse in a tight **chute** with a gate leading to the arena. The horse does not have enough freedom of motion to buck in the chute. Once the horse is released into the arena, it begins bucking immediately.

In bareback bronc riding, the cowboy holds on to a leather rigging, something like a briefcase handle on a strap. The rigging rides atop the horse's **withers**. It is secured with a **cinch**.

A bronco in bucking mode storms from the chute.

His arm taped for support, a bareback bronc rider grabs the rigging.

11

★ The flank strap wraps around
★ a bucking horse's midsection.

A saddle bronc rider competes from a special saddle, made without a saddle horn. Instead of a rigging, the saddle bronc rider grasps a long, thick **hack rein** that is attached to the horse's **halter**.

Bucking horses wear a **flank strap**. It is simply a band tied around the horse's flank. The idea is that the horse will buck to rid itself of the flank strap, as if having a rider aboard was not enough reason to buck!

Saddle bronc rider grips the hack rein.

Both saddle and bareback riders must be touching the horse's shoulders as it charges from the chute. The cowboy's feet must stay there until the horse has made its first jump, or buck, and returned to the ground. This riding technique is called a **mark out**.

If the cowboy fails to properly mark out, he is disqualified from the run.

Shifting positions of the cowboy's feet are critical in earning style points.

★ Successful mark out means
★ keeping the boots high on
★ the bronc's shoulders.

15

As the ride unfolds, the cowboy tries to point his boots outward. That turns the spurs on his heels inward toward the horse. A cowboy's or cowgirl's spurring action is a big part of bronc riding style.

The rider tries to use his spurs on the horse at several locations, from the points of the animal's shoulders to the back of the saddle. The better the spurring motion, as the judges see it, the better the score. The judges also want to see the rider's spurs consistently turned inward toward the horse.

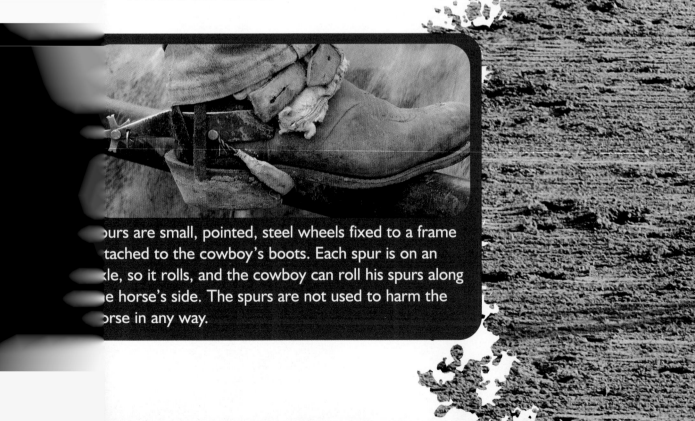

Spurs are small, pointed, steel wheels fixed to a frame attached to the cowboy's boots. Each spur is on an axle, so it rolls, and the cowboy can roll his spurs along the horse's side. The spurs are not used to harm the horse in any way.

Meanwhile, the cowboy struggles just to stay aboard. A saddle bronc cowboy must lift on the hack rein to balance himself in the saddle. The bareback rider grips the rigging.

Cowboys do not pick their broncs. The broncs are supplied to a rodeo by a **livestock contractor**. Some broncs, of course, perform better than others. A particularly active, acrobatic bronc is judged more highly than a less active one.

A saddle bronc rider strains on his hack rein.

Two judges watch a ride, and each judge may award up to 25 points for the horse and 25 points for the rider.

All in a day's work, an acrobatic bronc tosses its rider.

A rider, then, could earn a maximum of 100 points combined from the two judges. A ride score in the high 80s is good.

By rules of the event, bronc riders must keep one hand free from contact with the horse.

The Riders

Bronc riding is extremely difficult and dangerous. It requires strength, stamina, flexibility, and more than a little courage.

Injuries are common. A bucking horse has a tremendous amount of power and speed. It puts a great deal of stress on a rider's arm, especially the bareback rider. Bronc riders risk elbow, shoulder, lower back, neck, and spine injuries from their jarring rides. Any rider who is not physically prepared for the sport faces an extra risk.

 Although superstar rodeo rider Bonnie McCarroll was killed in a bronc riding performance in 1929 at the Pendleton Roundup in Oregon, accidental deaths in bronc riding events are extremely unusual.

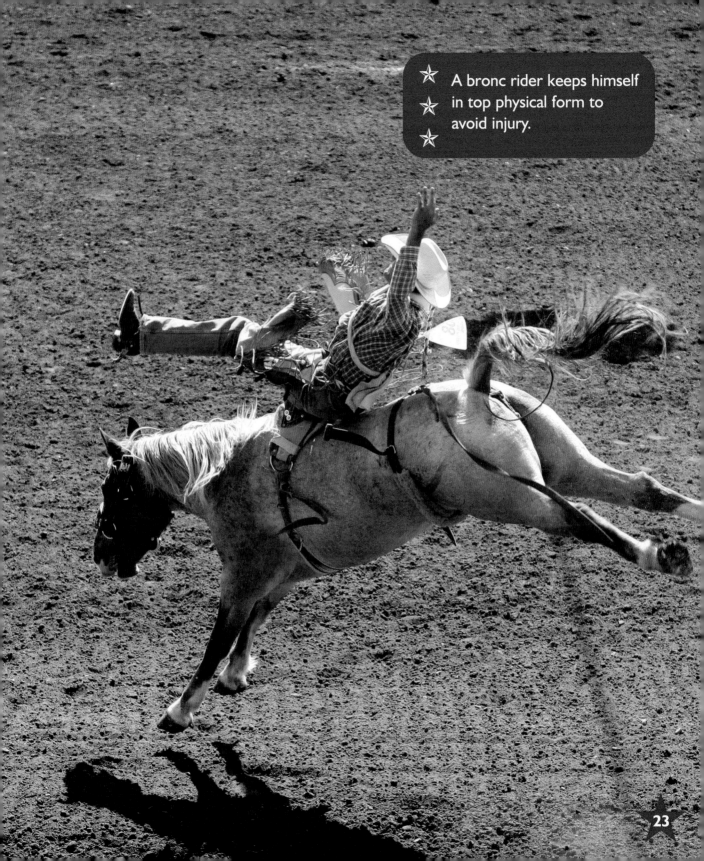

★ A bronc rider keeps himself
★ in top physical form to
★ avoid injury.

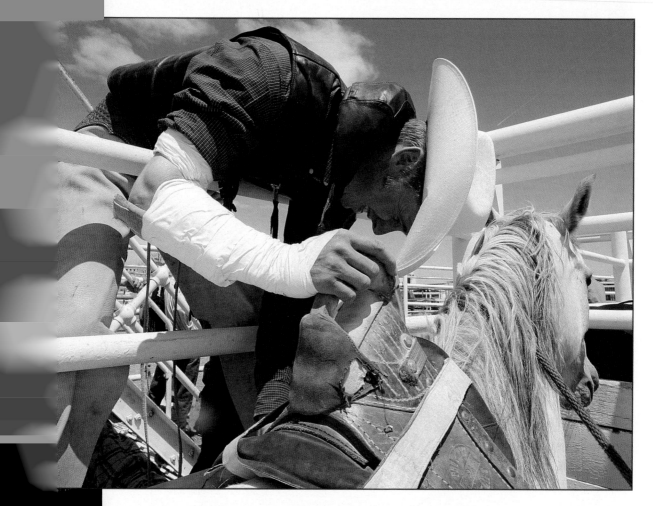

Bronc riders typically use tape and pressure brace to avoid over-extending their arms.

Ask Casey Tibbs, one of the greatest rodeo performers of all time, about injuries. The amazing Mr. Tibbs won six saddle bronc world championships, a bareback bronc world championship, and two all-around world championship titles. Tibbs' accomplishments were not without pain. He reportedly broke 46 bones during his career.

Another bareback bronc rider of special note is Chris Ledeoux, who died at the age of 57, in 2004. Ledeoux was a world champion bareback rider and a talented musician, poet, and sculptor.

Airborne, a bronc manages to throw its rider.

☆ Two of the most outstanding saddle bronc riders are Bill
☆ Etbauer, a world champ five times, and Dan Mortensen,
☆ six times a world champion. Etbauer won his fifth world
☆ title in 2004. Mortensen, now semiretired, was the world
☆ all-around champion in 1997. A year later he became the
☆ first cowboy to win more than $200,000 in a single event
☆ in one year's competition.

The Horses

Bucking horses are not wild horses, at least not in the sense of being animals that freely roam, like American **mustangs**. Bucking horses are raised on farms and ranches that specialize in breeding horses that will buck energetically if given the opportunity. If a horse does not buck well, it will be trained as a riding horse.

Bucking horses, like many of the men and women who ride them, travel from one rodeo to another by horse van. A bucking horse is never ridden more than once a day and never more than two days in a row. Like their riders, bucking horses need to be well rested and well fed to be at their best in the arena.

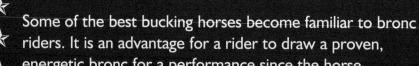

Some of the best bucking horses become familiar to bronc riders. It is an advantage for a rider to draw a proven, energetic bronc for a performance since the horse will be judged.

The best of broncs and bronc riders compete at PRCA's National Rodeo Finals in Las Vegas.

The History of Bronc Riding

Bronc riding is another of the rodeo sports that is like real ranch work. Taming, or breaking, young horses has been a necessity ever since human beings decided these sturdy animals just might be useful to them. Spanish explorers began bringing horses from Spain to the Americas in the late 15th century, so Mexicans, and eventually Americans, Canadians, and American Indians, have been breaking horses in North America for more than 500 years.

Having stayed aboard the bronc for eight seconds, a cowboy is taken off by rodeo pickup men.

Bronc riding has been a **cornerstone** of the American rodeo since rodeo events were first exhibited in a semiformal way in the late 1800s, with the likes of Buffalo Bill Cody's Wild West Show. Bronc riding will continue to be a rodeo cornerstone just as sure as cowboys wear boots.

★ Cowboys traditionally broke
★ horses by climbing on their
★ backs and letting them buck
★ until they were too tired to
★ buck any longer. That practice
★ became the foundation for
★ bronc riding in rodeos.

CHEYENNE FRONTIER DAYS

cfdrodeo.com

cf

29

Glossary

arena (uh-REE-nuh): the large enclosure in which rodeo and other events are held for public view

bronco (BRON-ko): a bucking horse

chute (SHOOT): a tight, high-sided space in which individual animals can be contained and kept apart from each other

cinch (SINCH): a tight strap that attaches under and around a horse or to a saddle

cornerstone (KOR-nur-stone): a basic part or foundation of something

flank strap (FLANGK STRAP): a band tied around a bronco's flanks to encourage bucking behavior

hack rein (HAK RAYN): a thick rope or strap attached to a horse's halter

halter (HAWL-tur): a rope or leather fixture for a horse's head and nose, for the purpose of leading or guiding

livestock contractor (LIVE-stok KON-trakt-ur): one who sells or leases horses or cattle for rodeo use

mark out (MARK OUT): a position that a bronc rider must take with his or her feet as the horse begins its first kick

mustangs (MUS-tangz): wild or feral horses, especially those with Spanish bloodlines

roughstock (RUHF-stok): referring to rodeo's judged events with broncos and bulls

withers (WITH-urz): the ridge at the upper base of the neck and between the shoulder bones of a horse

Further Reading

Want to learn more about rodeos? The following books and websites are a great place to start!

Books

Ehringer, Gavin. *Rodeo Legends: 20 Extraordinary Athletes of America's Sport*. Western Horseman, 2003.

Harris, Moira C. *Rodeo and Western Riding*. Book Sales, Inc., 2007.

Presnall, Judith Jada. *Rodeo Animals*. Gale Group, 2004.

Websites

http://www.wpra.com
http://prorodeo.org
www.nlbra.com

Index

About The Author

Lynn M. Stone is a widely published wildlife and domestic animal photographer and the author of more than 500 children's books. His book *Box Turtles* was chosen as Outstanding Science Trade Book and Selectors' Choice for 2008 by the Science Committee of the National Science Teachers' Association and the Children's Book Council.